A Little Girl's Gift

BY

LAWRENCE ELLIOTT

SCRIVANA PRESS

IOWA CITY • EUGENE

ISBN 978-0-9763016-5-3

Published by Scrivana Press
Iowa City, Iowa and Eugene, Oregon

Designed by Niki Harris

First edition © 1963 by Lawrence Elliott
Published in Canada and the United States
by Holt, Rinehart and Winston.

A portion of this book appeared originally
in *Reader's Digest* under the title,
"The Triumph of Janis Babson."

Available online from www.lulu.com
and other booksellers.

A Little Girl's Gift

FOREWORD

Fifty years have passed since Janis Babson died at the age of ten, with everything to live for. She was the second eldest of six children in a warm and loving family and, before she fell ill, she was slender and lithe and a blossoming beauty, and always among the brightest in her class. Her world, a small street in suburban Ottawa, with her school at one end and friends of all ages in virtually every house on the block, was endlessly fascinating to her and she responded to it with a full heart, draining every day of all it had to offer.

And yet when the end came, when she understood that she was going to die, she was not afraid; she *knew* she was going to be with God in heaven. Her one fear was that she would be forgotten, but of course that did not happen, and many generations will pass before it does. To this day, Janis is all but a living presence in the Babson family. And all unknowing, by her innocent certainty in the thing she had to do—by enabling two people to see through her own two eyes and thereby inspiring an unparalleled surge, not only in the numbers who pledged their eyes, but among a multitude of new donors who committed their corneal tissue, bone marrow and vital, life-giving organs to transplant centers around the world—Janis herself assured that she would live on in countless minds and hearts.

I came on the scene nearly two years later, an unfledged writer covering Canada and Alaska for *Reader's Digest*, on the hunt for tales of heroism and derring-do. I had heard about Janis' story—in those days it was hard to spend any time in Canada and not hear about her—but it sounded to me like a story more suited to *The Ladies Home Journal*. Still, in the dead of a Canadian winter, Ottawa, as compared, say, to Nome, Alaska, or Yellowknife in the Northwest Territories, sounded amenable. So one icy January evening I sat in the living room of that house on Cote de Neiges Road in City View and listened, rapt, as Rita and Rudy Babson talked about their lost daughter, and I knew it would be a long time before I found a story to match it.

I came back again and again, peppering Rita and Rudy with questions, all answered thoughtfully and with unfailing patience. I read the local press which, in the spring and summer of 1961, had been full of articles about Janis and the Ontario Division of the Eye Bank of Canada;

I talked to Janis' friends and teachers and doctors. And then, finally, I went home and started to write.

My story followed a course that ran directly counter to *Reader's Digest* practice which, in those days, normally abridged articles from other magazines or the writer's original text. "The Triumph of Janis Babson," as the *Digest* version was entitled, ran at full supplement length, 12,000 words, four times longer then the average article. But when the editors at Holt, Rinehart & Winston were sent a copy to consider for book publication, they said yes—if I could make it twice as long. That was not a problem; I had material, on paper and in my heart, for a second volume. And so *A Little Girl's Gift* was born.

The reviews were good; rights were bought by several publishers abroad. But when the first printing of 5000 copies was exhausted, no second printing was forthcoming. If I ever asked why, now, half a century later, I can't remember what I was told. Of course publishers are famous for their mistakes. *Gone With the Wind* was rejected by 38 of them; another wrote of a young author that "The girl doesn't have the special perception or feeling which would lift her book above the 'curiosity' level." The girl was Anne Frank.

Please accept that I am not comparing myself to Margaret Mitchell or Anne Frank, or my book to their two literary monuments. But it is a fact that to this day, people around the world have sought out members of the Babson family or me or another of those in the close circle of Janis torch-bearers, to ask where they could find a copy of the book, or to ask a question, or just to say "hello," or "I think about her all the time." If you Google Janis Babson on the Internet, on any given day you will find twelve to fifteen entries, many of them from people trying to find a copy of the book.

So here it is.

Still, I have to say that without the support and encouragement of the Babson family, with whom, over all these years, I have never lost touch, I would not have attempted this new edition. I am proud to be their friend. As Stephany says, Janis was the exceptional one, but Janis was in excellent company.

Lawrence Elliott
Luxembourg
December 2010

Introduction

I never knew my sister Janis. Now, as someone born five years after she died, I sit here wondering what I can tell anyone about her, and why this new edition of *A Little Girl's Gift* matters.

Janis left this world in 1961 at the age of ten after a two-year battle with leukemia. Her entire life was a gift to my family, for she radiated the joy that filled all her days. But she is remembered today for her gift to the Ontario Eye Bank—the corneal tissue she pledged so two blind people she would never know could see—and for everything that happened after that.

The idea came to her long before she died, from a television program she saw about how the blind in their thousands could be made to see if more people willed their corneal tissue to an eye bank. Then and there she told our mother that that's what she wanted to do, and she wasn't going to forget about it. And she didn't. On her death bed she made our parents promise that they would see to it.

Soon after, columnist Tim Burke of the *Ottawa Journal* wrote a touching story about Janis' brave struggle against leukemia and her selfless last wish. It rippled out on the wire services, generated more newspaper articles, and led to the inspirational little book, *Janis of City View,* by Holy Cross Sister Irene Primeau, under a pen name, Rena Ray. Meanwhile the Ontario Eye Bank was getting more pledges of corneal tissue in a week than it had ever before received in a year.

Then a writer, Lawrence Elliott, came to our house to talk with my mother and father, and what followed was a phenomenon, a medium on a totally different level through which Janis could weave her magic. First, in June, 1963, there came Larry Elliott's *Reader's Digest* article, "The Triumph of Janis Babson," which went out around the world in 28 million copies and 13 different languages. Later that year, his book, *A Little Girl's Gift,* the expanded version of the article, was published and added fuel to the growing worldwide interest in corneal, organ and bone marrow transplants.

A ten-year-old girl in Longview, Texas, read it and never forgot it. Years later, by then a married mother of two, she helped to organize a walk-a-thon on behalf of two local youths ill with leukemia to publicize the search for donors with compatible bone marrow. Amy Hill had heard the call and went on working to promote marrow donation and marrow banks. The idea, popularized as the Because I Care campaign, spread across the state, across the country, around the world and, under different names, continues to save lives.

Sparking interest in organ transplantation, generating studies in leukemia research and inspiring young people to pursue medical, spiritual and professional goals, my sister Janis has been changing lives ever since her own was cut so short. A little girl's gift, indeed.

She was very much part of my life. Some of my earliest memories have to do with her legacy. I remember leafing through our copies of the articles and books about her and reading them endlessly as I grew older, never quite believing that this amazing little girl was my sister. In our living room we had shelves of *Reader's Digest* issues in languages from around the world, every one featuring the now famous picture of my sister's beautiful smile. I used her tiny green sewing machine for my dolls' clothes and drew pictures on the blank pages of her perfectly scripted and organized school workbooks, filled with praise from her teachers. I remember coming across the colouring book in which she had written the sad words, quoted in this book, of her homesickness in the hospital and her love and longing for our parents.

Most of all I remember the letters. My parents had organised scrapbooks and scrapbooks filled with letters from people around the world, but their sheer numbers were daunting and soon there were sacks full as well: notes from kids who wanted to be like Janis and who had adopted her as their new best friend; letters from adults who told how her story had lifted them and how they now meant to live their lives differently, in both large and small ways. Many wanted to meet our family, believing that we must be truly extraordinary to have nurtured someone like Janis. I sometimes felt that people idealized us, which made me uncomfortable. We were and are normal people, and actually pretty ordinary. Janis was the exceptional one.

My siblings and I were typical kids. Even when Janis was ill, my brothers and sisters didn't really treat her any differently. They were unfamiliar with serious sickness and among their memories of Janis are times when they were mean to her or indifferent to the reality of what was happening. Rod remembers snapping an elastic band at her, as little brothers do, and being swept with guilt when she cried out in pain. Karen, always mischievous, once ripped the heads off her cardboard dolls, to which Janis responded with a little note: "Dear Karen, you are so bad! But I will always love you."

Memories like that leave lasting imprints, and especially on children. To see a sibling suffer and die is an alien experience. As Rod once put it, dying is "something that old people do." My brothers and sisters have been very honest with me in describing their feelings of guilt about Janis and her death, admitting to feelings of jealousy because she was receiving so much attention, not understanding the reality of why this was so. Karen remembers, in a particularly painful way, having such feelings on May 12, 1961. It was her fifth birthday and, seeing all the cars arriving at our house, assuming everyone was coming to help her celebrate, she was full of excitement. But in fact the people were coming to support my parents, for Janis had just died. The emotional mix of guilt and grief, love and loss, is a difficult set of emotions. There were no shrines for Janis, but each of my sisters and brothers mourns her privately and in her and his own way.

In the late 1980s, when I was studying television broadcasting, I produced a documentary film about Janis, which was later submitted to CBC Telefest. It was my first video production of substance and was amateurish and created with no budget. I cringe looking at it now, but the raw power of the interview clips shines through. I interviewed everyone who had a connection to Janis, from my mother to Susan Perkins, the little girl Janis helped in the hospital—who eventually made a complete recovery from her leukemia.

The interviews with Charmaine were heartbreaking. As the eldest sibling, she has the sharpest memories of that time and it was particularly painful for her to be taken back there and have them stirred awake. But she did it for me, and for Janis. She told me about the time she had accompanied our father, Rudy, and Janis to the hospital where Janis was to undergo a bone marrow aspiration, a terribly painful procedure. Charmaine was delighted with the toys and books in the waiting room and proceeded to amuse herself as Janis and my dad disappeared next door. Thoroughly immersed in her little pleasures, it took her some minutes to process the screams from beyond the closed door as coming from her sister. She heard Janis cry out, "Oh, dear Jesus, you were once a child! Please, please help me!" A lifetime later the door opened and my father came out carrying Janis. Both were white with exhaustion.

Today, Charmaine says, "Janis is in my deepest thoughts and everyday joys and has always been there. She gives me focus and hope when I can't always get there by myself."

Now Sally has taken up the cause. She was only two when Janis died and has no memories of our sister. But she is the one who now regularly Googles Janis' name and corresponds with the many people in cyberspace who are still talking about that ten-year-old girl who willed her eyes to the eye bank. She is currently working on setting up a web site for Janis and our family. Recently, her efforts led to a shipment of daffodil bulbs to us, the "Narcissus Janis Babson," created in honour of my sister by Murray W. Evans in Oregon.

The daffodils, the letters, the phone calls are among the wide-ranging signs of the impact Janis still has on the world half a century after her death. Some others:

• Fern Tremblay, president and CEO of the Joseph Fortin Foundation in Timmins, Ontario, and a driving force in boosting the numbers of corneal and organ donations, championed the distribution of "The Triumph of Janis Babson" to all Catholic schools in Timmins.

• A Canadian artist, Caroline Langill, inspired by Janis' life and death, created an installation called "Custody of the Eyes" at the Ottawa Art Gallery.

• Lidiane Berbert, a young Brazilian, after reading Janis' story as a child, decided to become a doctor. Today she works for Doctors Without Borders.

• Another doctor, Emily Polis Gibson, also decided on her profession when still a child because of Janis. Telling about it on her internet blog, she wrote, "I cried buckets of tears, reading about that death scene. My mom finally had to take the magazine away from me and shooed me outside to run off my grief."

Every week for the first year or so after Janis' death, my parents would pack everyone into the car to visit the grave. But as the years passed so did the time between visits. But of course we still go occasionally, planting flowers, clearing the spiders away from the statue of Ste. Therese, each of us to say a few private words.

In 1975, at 52 years of age, our wonderful father Rudy died of a sudden heart attack and now shares the gravesite with Janis. I was eight at the time but the pain is still raw and visiting the graves is an overwhelming experience for me. Maybe Janis knew that Dad would be taken early and sent me to help my mom. She and I have leaned on each other ever since his death. She gave me my middle name, Theresa, in honour of Janis' "big sister in heaven."

Our mother, Rita, is not only hale and hearty, she is incredible. She has lost a child, her husband, her parents and younger siblings but still remains a source of strength, a gentle soul who is tough as nails. We love her to distraction. Now in her eighties, she is still beautiful, with pale green eyes and her trademark red hair.

After Dad's death, she and I moved back to Cape Breton, Nova Scotia, for a period, but now she lives in Ottawa, to be near Dad, Janis and her memories. Cold Ottawa winters cannot keep her away from mass, as she has always had a solid and unwavering faith. She has six great-grandchildren and I am sure there will be more to come. She lives in an apartment surrounded by little touches of Janis—a stuffed red velvet heart, trimmed with faded white lace that Janis hand-stitched, and a needlework piece that features a little house and the words "God Bless Our Home." Janis never had the chance to finish it, so it was finished by Sally, who has inherited Grandmother Babson's skill with a needle. A large, beautiful painting of Janis sits above the rocking chair where Mom spends many hours. It is the same chair my dad used to relax in after work while, as a little girl, I would massage his sore feet. Often, something in a conversation will remind Mom of Janis and she will trail off and say, "Your sister Janis…" And then her voice will drop to a whisper as she speaks directly to Dee Dee, the family nickname for Janis.

Charmaine and Sally still live in Ottawa, with their respective partners. Charmaine has three children, the eldest of whom is named Janis Anne, and two granddaughters. She is now retired from a long career with the RCMP Forensic Investigation Unit. Sally is senior events manager at Carleton University.

Rod is married and lives near Belleville, Ontario, and is the proud father of an adult son and daughter. Always the technical one, he has built two of his houses from the ground up, and works in the telecommunications field. Tim, who is retired from the Canadian armed forces, is settled in Edmonton. He was always fascinated with the military and my childhood is filled with memories of his model tanks and his incredible ability to whistle bagpipes tunes.

Karen and I both live in Toronto. Karen has two red-headed sons, perpetuating the lineage of the redheads from our mom and Grandma Quinn, and four grand-sons. She's the family sales whiz, and works as a retail manager. I am a writer and video producer/director.

I often wonder what Janis would have chosen for a pro-fession; she once mentioned to my mother that she would like to be a nun. She was so mature and wise for one so young. If she had been given the years to grow, I feel sure her contribution to the world would have been something wonderful. Of course her contribution was truly wonder-ful—and she took less than eleven years to accomplish it. We should all be so fortunate in our life's work!

It gives us great peace to know that people around the world are still being touched by Janis, as she was con-cerned about being forgotten. Read her story and share it with those you care about. She will smile in heaven. And she may just change your life.

The Babsons want to thank Larry Elliott for the hon-est deep feeling he has put into Janis' story, and for spear-heading this new edition of *A Little Girl's Gift*. He is a good man and a good friend.

Stephany Babson
Toronto
November 2010

Her name was Janis —

"With an *s*," she would gravely inform you—and that winter of 1959 she was eight years old. Her hair was darkening from its color of gold. She was slender and lithe. When she laughed, her eyes shone with an inner light of happiness, and life welled up so strongly in her that sometimes it bubbled over.

"Gosh, Mom, it's *fun*!" she sang out one January afternoon, as she flew into the house.

"What's fun?" her mother asked.

"Everything! School and all the snow and playing with the kids. Oh, you know—everything!"

She had been born in Windsor, Nova Scotia, on September 9, 1950. Her father, a member of the Royal Canadian Mounted Police, had been stationed in that ruggedly lovely maritime province for many years, at various detachments charged with the patrolling of hundreds of miles of lonely coastline and rocky interior. From 1944 to 1946, Constable Rudy Babson's assignment had been to work with a highly trained police dog; he and his charges had searched out lost children, smugglers, and fleeing criminals. Often, his assignments would take him into the wilds for days at a time.

In the fall of 1945, Rudy met Rita Quinn, whose family had worked in the bleak Nova Scotia coal mines for as long as she could remember. Rita was pretty and vivacious and had dark red hair; it wasn't long before she and the tall Mountie were a familiar couple at the only movie theater in Truro and at the occasional RCMP dance. They were married in Sydney Mines, Rita's home town, in June, 1948, and their first home was a kitchen and living room apartment, the only available accommodation in the tiny community of Sheet Harbour. Here, Charmaine, first of the Babson children, was born in May, 1949. The landlord was so delighted by the pert new arrival that he rented the little family an additional bedroom.

Janis was born the next year, and when she was fifteen months old, Rudy received transfer orders. His new assignment was the Identification Branch at Mountie headquarters in Ottawa. On Christmas Eve, in 1951, the Babsons moved into a neat gray stucco house on a quiet street in the suburb of City View, just southwest of Ottawa. That house, that street, became Janis Babson's world, and she loved it openly, exuberantly.

Down the road was the brand new ten-room St. Nicholas Separate School. As a toddler, Janis used to trip gaily down that road wearing her mother's make-up, fancy hat askew and high heels clacking—one day to come running home to report breathlessly that the workmen had told her the new school belonged to Santa Claus. "Honest, Mom; they said it's to be St. Nicholas' school!"

Now Janis was in third grade, tied in an earnest rivalry with Elizabeth Hayes for top spot in the class. Beyond the school stretched a farm where, long ago, Janis had been completely captivated by the fine hackney show horses. You could see her almost any afternoon, skipping down the street with a gift of carrots swinging from her clenched hand. Rita Babson once told Rudy that the only way she could keep carrots in the house was to hide them. When Janis overheard her mother telling a neighbor of the long hours the little girl spent just hanging over that farm fence, Janis, in all seriousness, said, "I wouldn't *have* to go down there. If you let me keep one of the horses in the garage, I'd never ever leave the house."

Hers was an endlessly beguiling world. There was Tricia Kennedy, her very best friend, who lived down the street; and Suzie the beagle right next door. There were books filled with the magic of faraway places, and the creation of dances and plays to stage with Charmaine, and water colors and knitting, and a boy with a crew cut, named Ronnie, who had smiled at her during Little League games the summer before.

Each wakening day was a gift. So was the awesome sense of discovery at the sight of spring's first robin—"Look, Daddy! Oh, look! It's right on *our* lawn!" Sometimes, on her knees, Janis thanked her dear God for all the good things in her world. That's the kind of little girl she was.

She didn't *feel* spiritual. She wouldn't even have understood the word. It was just that God was very close to her, a part of her everyday life. She *knew* Him. He was real.

Her feelings were special, but she was far from starchy or self-righteous about them. The fact is that a healthy curiosity and irrepressible spirit sometimes landed her in hot water typical of other life-loving children. One day, she and Charmaine went to call for Tina Stanfield, a little neighbor friend. No one answered their knock, but finding the door ajar, they wandered in, feeling terribly adventurous—and only a little self-conscious—in the familiar house, now suddenly vast and hollow-sounding. Looking in the refrigerator, they oohed and aahed over fresh apples and home-made ice cream, succumbing, finally, and helping themselves to generous quantities of each. Wandering upstairs to the bathroom they found some lipstick, and inexpertly daubed their lips, noses, and cheeks, accidentally dumping over a full box of bath powder in their enthusiasm.

It was at this critical moment that they heard the downstairs door open. They froze. Mrs. Stanfield was saying, "Who in the world left the refrigerator door open?" They dared not breathe.

Conscience-stricken, panic-stricken, and desperately wishing themselves somewhere else, or at the least invisible, the girls fled to a bedroom, squirming behind the dresses in a clothes closet to hide. But they had plainly marked their every step with well-powdered footprints. It was only a matter of moments before, inevitably, they heard Mrs. Stanfield say, sounding like the voice of doom, "Well, well, and what have we here?"

Caught dead to rights, the young culprits were returned to their home, solemnly given a lecture, and sent to their room by their parent; but for a long time afterward, the older Babsons and Stanfields laughed themselves teary-eyed over the girls' real-life re-creation of the story of the three bears.

Now there were five Babson children other than Janis—Charmaine, nearly two years older; and Roddy, Karen, Timmy, and Sally, who were all younger. The babies, Timmy and Sally, were a very special joy. Janis called them "the small fry," and to them she was Dee-Dee, the name Charmaine had given to her when still too young to cope with pronouncing Janis.

After church on Sunday, Janis often persuaded her mother to dress the small fry in their best and prop them in a carriage and, her own head barely poking above the handle, she'd push them from one end of the Cote de Neiges Road to the other. She beamed with pride when neighbors stopped to admire her little brother and sister. "They're very naughty," she'd gravely inform them, then burst into that sun-warm grin. "But, oh, are they ever cute!"

Her feelings ran deep. She cried with happiness when Sally was born and, in the last, difficult months just before birth, she was constantly urging Rita to rest more. "Sit down and put your feet up, Mom, please. I can start the supper." It made her sad, she later told her mother, to see Sally growing up. "She might be our last baby," she said, with that sixth sense with which sensitive children are sometimes gifted.

When Rita bought a new dress or hat, Janis would hop up and down with excitement, no less proud than if it were her very own. "Are you going to wear it to the church supper, Mom, are you? You'll look beautiful!"

When she had a row with Charmaine, as sisters inevitably must, Janis remained deeply upset until they made up. "I can never have a good argument with her," Charmaine once told her mother good-naturedly. "She takes it so seriously."

Janis worried about the birds getting enough to eat in winter. Or how her grandmother in far-off Fort William was managing alone. "Can she get somebody at least to help her carry the wood in?" Stirred by something she'd read, her eyes would mist over. Each time she heard the story of the Crucifixion, it wounded her anew, as though it had happened only that morning. Once she said, "Why do people ever have to be mean to each other? I wish I could be everybody-in-the-world's best friend."

One day, during White Cane Week, Canada's great annual effort in behalf of the blind, Janis was watching a television program about the Eye Bank. The announcer explained how it was at this time possible to help many blind people to see again by performing a surgical transplant of healthy corneal film, the fingernail-sized tissue that covers the iris and pupil. If donated by someone who had died, the transplant could be made to the eyes of perhaps two people with corneal disease or damage. Then, a young mother appeared on the program to tell how she had lost her child in an accident, and how she had bequeathed his eyes so that a stranger could see. It gave her solace, the mother said. In the restored vision of someone she'd never known, as in her own heart, the little boy lived on.

The program affected Janis deeply. Long after it was over, she still sat before the darkened set, silent and thoughtful. Finally, she went out to the kitchen.

"Mom," she said softly, "when I die, I'm going to give my eyes to the Eye Bank."

Rita put down the potato she was peeling. She would later remember that her first reaction was the same as if Janis had just said she wanted to visit the moon. But Rita Babson didn't laugh or dismiss her child. And if there was an impatient remark on her lips, she quelled it, a fact for which she would be forever grateful. For tears stood in her daughter's eyes as she told what she had seen on television. "They could help so many more—Mom, there are thousands and thousands of blind people just waiting their turn! If only everyone pledged their eyes."

Rita had listened intently, and she was moved. But how do you respond to a child who, out of her compassion, stands so confidently ready to make such a far-reaching promise. Did she really know what she was saying?

"I know how you feel, dear," Rita finally said. "But that's such a serious decision for a little girl. Don't you think you'd better wait awhile? You might want to change your mind when you're older."

Janis shook her head emphatically. "I'll always feel the

same," she said firmly. Her head down during a long moment of thought, she added at last, "And I'm not going to forget about it either, Mom."

There was a lot of snow that February. For Janis, it was an enchanted time. She was outdoors every afternoon, whirling down the hill on her "flying saucer," building great ice forms with Tricia Kennedy and the other girls, and waging epic—and giggly—snowball warfare with the boys on the block. Charmaine, and then Roddy, both of whom had winter colds, watched enviously from the dining-room window; and Janis, when she finally came in, reluctant, red-cheeked, and still full of the day's adventures, usually brought an armful of delicately shaped icicles as gifts for them. Huddled around the bathtub, the three youngsters conjured up spires and statues until the last sliver had melted.

And then, all of a sudden, Janis seemed to run out of steam. A few minutes of play left her totally spent. She yawned and sighed heavily, usually too tired to manage more than a few mouthfuls of dinner. Rita Babson thought it was surely Janis' turn to be coming down with a cold—"Timmy and Karen next, and then we'll be finished with *that* for the winter," she told Rudy with a wry smile—though Janis had neither temperature nor sniffles, only that great weariness which wouldn't go away.

As February slipped into March, shadows darkened under her eyes. Her head ached, and sometimes the smell of cooking food sickened her. One night, while she did her homework, she snapped erect in her chair and cried out, "Oh, that hurt!"

"What hurt? What's the matter?" her mother asked, alarmed.

"My back," was the slow reply. "It's okay now, but it sure hurt for a second."

Despite Rita's worried entreaties that she rest for a few days, Janis wouldn't think of staying home from school. "And let Elizabeth Hayes get ahead of me? Oh, please, Mom. I'm not *that* sick."

And, indeed, she didn't seem to be. Surely there was no specific symptom to indicate anything seriously wrong. Rita decided that perhaps Janis needed some iron pills, and Rudy made preparations to leave for the RCMP Training Division at Rockcliffe, north of Ottawa, for a general refresher course the following week.

But on a particularly stormy afternoon, when Janis hadn't come home from school with Charmaine and Roddy, Rita, watching from the dining-room window, saw Janis battling her way up the street. She was chilled by the sight. Arms loaded with books, the frail figure had to push forward through the snow one slow, painful step at a time, sometimes stopping for a long moment, as though gathering her strength, sometimes blown almost to her knees by the force of the wind.

"Roddy!" Rita called tensely. "Run out and help Dee-Dee home! Hurry!"

The seven-year-old threw on his coat and dashed out. He ran up to his sister and took her books. Walking in front of her to break the wind's fierce drive, he led the way up the street and around the deepest drifts. Rita, still watching, noticed that Janis had to cling to the back of Roddy's coat to support herself.

"Whew!" Janis gasped limply when they came in. "I don't know what happened. I just—I couldn't walk anymore." She slumped heavily into a chair. "Mom, I'm so tired."

Rita quickly slipped off Janis' coat. She looked closely at the little girl, and was suddenly frightened by her pallor and the way the brown eyes now seemed to fill Janis' thin face. Even Roddy grew anxious.

"What's the matter, Dee-Dee? Are you sick?"

Janis shook her head. "Just tired," she insisted. But it came out as barely a whisper.

When Rudy Babson came home that evening, Rita told him what had happened. "I think we'd better have Dr. Whillans look at Janis before you leave for Rockcliffe," she said. "Rudy, I'm worried."

Though concerned now himself, Rudy tried to reassure his wife. "It's probably just some kid thing," he told her. "There's nothing to worry about."

But later that night he slipped into Janis' room to gaze silently at the sleeping child, and next afternoon he left work early to take her to the office of Dr. James A. Whillans, the family pediatrician.

They sat in the waiting room, the big Mountie corporal and the pale child. It was to be the first of many such long times, of many waiting rooms for the two of them. And if Janis drew strength from the comfort of her father's calm presence, Rudy, in days to come, was to gain strength from his little girl's courage.

When they were ushered inside the examining room, Dr. Whillans, a young and enthusiastic physician, said, "Well, young lady, is this a new way of getting out of school?"

Janis grinned and brought a laugh to the two men when she answered, "No, it's a new way for Daddy to get out of work."

Rudy Babson remembers the moment vividly. "It was my last honest laugh for a long time," he has said.

He watched Dr. Whillans peer into his daughter's throat and ears and listen to the beat of her heart. Then, studying a blood smear through his microscope, Whillans stiffened, as though it were hard for him to believe what he saw. He looked again and said, "Will you let the nurse stick your finger again, Janis?"

When he had examined the second smear, Whillans spoke to Rudy Babson. "Her hemoglobin seems unusually low." He was lost in thought for a moment and Rudy stared at him blankly.

"What does that mean?" the Mountie finally asked.

"Hemoglobin is a substance in the red blood cells," the doctor said carefully. "When it drops, it usually indicates an anemic condition, maybe that the white cells are building up for some reason. The question is: why?" He paused, then added, "I think it would be a good idea to have some fancy blood work done at a lab. How do you feel about that?"

Rudy looked back at the doctor from across the desk, searching his face intently. A moment before, they had been laughing together. Now, suddenly, there was much he wanted to ask, much he feared. But he only said, "Whatever you think, Doctor."

Neither Rudy nor Rita speculated aloud through the next long and anxious days, but both were much lost in thought. Rudy was granted permission to postpone his training course at Rockcliffe and, on Friday of that same week, he drove Janis to a medical laboratory, where a great many specimens were taken from her veins and fingers.

Trying hard not to wince, Janis asked, "Why do you have to fill so many different tubes? Isn't my blood the same, no matter where it comes from?"

"Umm, not quite, honey," the technician answered; then grinned at her. "Besides, we've got lots of tests to make and we don't want to run short. You wouldn't want us to send somebody around to knock at your door and say, 'Excuse me, Miss, but could you spare a cup of blood?'"

Janis squealed with delight at the joke, but Rudy's best effort was a thin smile.

Early Saturday morning Dr. Whillans telephoned. "Look," he said to Rudy brusquely, "I'm not very happy about this. I want you to get Janis up to the hospital—right away. I'm arranging for a blood specialist to see her."

Rudy Babson was alone in the kitchen, and still he spoke softly into the receiver, as though his very words were fraught with danger. "It couldn't be leukemia, could it, Doctor?"

For a moment, only electronic whisperings filled the line. Then Dr. Whillans' voice came back. "It could," he said.

Janis cried when her parents told her she would have to go to the hospital. "But I'm not really sick," she pleaded. "Honest, I'm just tired."

"Janis, dear," Rita said tenderly, "the doctor has to find out *why* you're tired. They can do that best in the hospital. They can give you medicine to make you better."

Janis fretted about missing school. She worried that the small fry would forget all about her if she went away. But in the end she quit crying and went up to her room to get her things. When Rita came up a few minutes later, she found Janis on her knees saying her rosary. Then she was ready to go.

The Ottawa Civic Hospital is a sprawling complex of red brick and glass buildings, nurses bustling, and visitors looking distracted and stiff in the waiting rooms. Janis felt small and lost there. But she was through with tears, and resolutely followed the admitting nurse down the long corridor to the children's ward.

When Rita and Rudy went in to tell her goodbye, Janis was wearing a little white hospital gown and sitting cross-legged on her bed, shyly studying the other children in the big white room. She managed a bright smile for her parents, but when they embraced her she whispered anxiously, "You'll come back to see me, won't you?"

"Of course, darling," Rita reassured her.

They came nearly every day, Rita in the afternoon whenever she could manage it and, usually, together each evening. They brought notes from Charmaine and scrawly drawings from Karen, which Janis exulted over and proudly displayed to her new friends in the ward. She passed the long days playing with the other little girls and shaping funny animals from tissues. These she sent home for the small fry, sometimes stuffing them with candies and the treats the nurses brought for her.

Janis reported that someone was there to take blood specimens from her fingers nearly every time she turned around. "I'm beginning to feel like a pin cushion," she laughed. "But if you look away and think of something different, it hardly hurts at all."

Janis was now in the care of Dr. Alexander English, one of Ottawa's leading hematologists. He promised a report as soon as possible. For the Babsons, it was a tense time, days of waiting for the telephone to ring and restless nights of worrying what the message might be.

At work, Rudy had to force himself just to perform his most routine tasks. During the drive home from RCMP headquarters in Overbrook each evening, he tried to imagine himself opening the front door and hearing Rita's voice, cheery and gay, the way it used to be before Janis became ill. "It's all right!" she'd be calling to him. "It was just a cold!"

Or an iron deficiency, or the flu—anything but that dread disease that was painful even to think about.

For Rita the hours were no less clouded. She made an effort to busy herself with the other children, household tasks, a magazine. But each time the telephone rang, it was as though she had lived all her life for that single electric instant, as she ran to snatch up the receiver. But it was never Dr. English.

Even Charmaine, now nearly ten, though she had been told only that Janis needed a "check-up," sensed the depth of the trouble. "Don't worry, Mom," she said toward the end of one particularly bleak afternoon. "Janis will be all right. I'm *sure* of it."

Rita clasped the child to her. "Of course she will," she whispered huskily. "You bet she will."

It was on Thursday night, only a little while after they'd returned from visiting Janis, that Dr. English did call. He asked Rudy and Rita if they would come back to the hospital. He was now able to give them a report, he said.

Rudy immediately began pulling on his coat. Rita just stood next to the hall closet, fingers pressing against her cheek. Finally, she said, "You go alone, all right? I—just can't. I'll wait for you."

"All right," Rudy said. He understood. He smiled encouragement, touched her arm, and went out.

After the children were in bed a neighbor came over to chat. "You're a good soldier," she said. "And it's going to be all right, wait and see."

When she'd gone, Rita flipped through the pages of a magazine. Then she turned the television set on, but the images were blurred to her eyes and the words seemed tasteless, absurd. And so, at last, she turned the set off and just sat waiting in the new stillness. That was hardest of all, but there was nothing else she could do, not until Rudy came home.

"It's leukemia," Dr. English said, as soon as he'd closed the door behind the tall, tense Mountie. "There's no easy way to say it, is there? I'm sorry. We've done a thorough study and there isn't any question about it."

He was an intense, medium-sized man, but his eyes looked very tired, and Rudy remembers thinking that it was probably a terribly discouraging job, terribly hard for this fine doctor, to have to make that grim little pronouncement to different parents day after day, to have to get to know an unending line of children who must soon die. Rudy sank into a chair, for now—and all in a rush— it had come over him that his child, Janis, would die.

"I'm sorry," Dr. English said again.

"There's no—chance?"

The doctor shook his head. "Not for what you're asking," he said kindly. "It's always fatal. But she has what we call a subacute form of the disease, and I don't think she's had it too long. With good care and the medicines we now have, the prognosis is good. She can live a year, maybe more. You have to make the most of that. "

Rudy nodded numbly. He wanted to say something to show that he understood and that he was grateful to this man, who looked suddenly so sad and tired, who was able to offer him only these few more months of life for his daughter. But, of course, there weren't any words.

"You're absolutely free to take her anywhere you like," Dr. English was saying. "But I'm certain of the diagnosis and there isn't a hospital in Canada—or the States—that knows any more about treating leukemia than we do. We're all in the same boat. We do the best we can; but there are no miracle cures. Don't go looking for them. It would only be a needless expense, and hard on the child."

Rudy nodded. "Whatever you think," he said.

English told him that once they had worked out the precise medication and were able to bring Janis' blood into better balance, she would be able to go home. He would need to keep a continuing check on her cell count. For this, Rudy was to bring her to the cancer clinic in the hospital each week.

"Otherwise, she can do what she's always done: go to school, play with her friends—everything. We'll have to put her on a salt-free diet, but there is absolutely no need to tell her any more than that she has something wrong with her blood and that we're treating it. She has a long, rough road ahead. Our job is to smooth out as many bumps as we can."

At the door Rudy turned back. "Will she suffer—later?" he asked.

"She might," English answered. Then he looked away.

The shushing sound of his tires was loud in Rudy's ears as he drove through the melting snow in the dark. He tried very hard to think of a way to break the news to Rita, some special words that might cushion the force of the blow.

But Rita was studying his face as he walked into the quiet house. Before he could even speak, she said, "It's leukemia, isn't it?"

"Yes," he said.

And so it was out.

They sat together on the couch and cried a little.

The Rita got up and made some coffee. They talked,

then fell silent, and talked some more, far into the night.

"We have to be strong, you and I," Rita said. "We have to give Janis strength."

They would, of course, not tell the other children. Janis was to live as happy and normal a life as they could provide for her in the time she had left. That much was settled. For the rest, they would bear it somehow. But later, in the stillness of their bedroom, they faced, separately and alone, the hard question of why did it have to be?

Janis was in the hospital for more than a month, improving steadily as various drugs were tested and the right ones took hold and fought back against the ravages of the disease. Heartened by her progress, she scurried around the children's ward, making friends with the other youngsters and completely captivating nurses and interns with her sunny, "Anything I can do to help today?"

One day a younger girl, Susie, was brought to Janis' room. She seemed very ill, and when she finally dropped off to sleep late in the afternoon Janis hushed the other youngsters with a whispered, "She needs to rest."

Susie woke, lonely and frightened, and Janis hurried to her bed. She would be her very special friend, she told the white-faced little girl. "You won't have to call the nurses if you need anything. Just tell me. Shall I read you a story?"

And so she read the story, and brought her the bedpan and innumerable drinks of water, and helped feed her at mealtimes. Each day, before visiting hours, she straightened Susie's bed and combed her hair, and said, "Now, remember, no crying when your mother and father get here. They have plenty to worry about without *that*."

It was during those weeks that Rita and Rudy acquired an intimate knowledge of leukemia. They learned that it is considered a kind of cancer, concentrating its attack on the organs that manufacture blood. For some medically unfathomable reasons, the lymphatic glands and bone marrow in Janis' body had gone berserk and were producing leukocytes, white blood cells, at a fantastic rate, driving the hemoglobin, or red-cell count, down to a dangerously low level. This was the disturbing clue first spotted by Dr. Whillans. A normal leukocyte count would have been perhaps 7,500 per cubic millimeter. Dr. English's examination showed the leukocyte count in Janis' blood to have been a hundred times that number.

Ordinarily, one of the main missions of these white blood cells, produced by the bone marrow and spleen, is to fight infection and disease. Healthy leukocytes produce antibodies, which seek out and destroy viruses and bacteria. In leukemia, however, the white cells are flawed, somehow, and instead of maturing to the point where they can perform these vital defensive duties, they turn on the body itself, spreading wildly, invading healthy tissue, breaking it down, and raging on. Constantly reinforced by the senseless and massive leukemic cell production of the marrow, they force the breakdown of the hemoglobin in the red cells, causing weakness, anemia, bleeding, and, inevitably, death.

By the time leukemia can be recognized, it is incurable. All that the best medical care can provide is treatment for the course of the dread disease, with the goal of keeping the patient as comfortable as possible for as long as possible. Toward this end, much progress has been made. The Babsons soon grew familiar with strange words like methotrexate and prednisone, for these are among the most useful of the new drugs employed in the battle against the invariable course of leukemia. Some of the drugs are cell poisons, and work by posing as essential vitamins to be quickly—and fatally—absorbed by the ravenous leukocytes. Some make a direct attack on the defective white cells. All are dangerously toxic and, despite the most cautious administration, do some damage to the bone marrow. Meanwhile, though, one or another of these drugs, carefully managed, can produce partial, even complete, remission of leukemia's symptoms. Blood transfusions, when necessary, build up the red cells to fight anemia and prevent hemorrhaging.

Finally, the Babsons learned the grimmest fact of all. Gradually, each course of treatment loses its effectiveness. Inevitably, the wild leukocyte multiplication begins anew. Having produced one remission, no drug is apt to be of any further use, unless given in such huge doses as to produce deadly side effects. In the end, none of the drugs would be of any help at all; nothing would.

To confirm his diagnosis and help him in weighing the effectiveness of the different drugs, Dr. English was forced to do several bone marrow aspirations—inserting a long needle from Janis' hip into her pelvis, or directly into the breastbone, and drawing out blood marrow for analysis—for the ordinary finger prick to get a blood sample wouldn't yield the detailed information he needed. It was a harrowing and agonizingly painful procedure, and Janis trembled with the memory of it for hours. To Rita and Rudy, however, she said only, "I can stand anything that helps make this silly blood of mine better."

Day by day, drugs were tested, their value assessed, and dosages adjusted. Finally, Janis' treatment was stabilized: so many pills of methotrexate, a nitrogen mustard, so many of prednisone, a steroid hormone. Quickly, she adjusted to the regimen and by mid-April she was in nearly full remission. She could go home!

It was one of those rare spring days, warm with the promise of summer, green stirrings everywhere. For Janis, the trip home was like a rediscovery of the world, and she gloried in it.

"Ooooh, everything's so pretty!" she exclaimed. "Even the potholes seem softer."

By the time the Babsons turned into Cote de Neiges Road, she was bouncing with excitement and straining to catch sight of a familiar face. When she saw Tricia Kennedy waiting in front of the gray stucco house, she all but flew from the car.

"Tricia! I'm home! Oh, gosh, Trish, I'm going to blubber!"

Rita Babson watched the two girls embrace. She saw lively new color in her daughter's cheeks and the spirit with which Janis bolted up the steps to greet her brothers and sisters. And she thought that it must all have been a bad dream. Janis was not really going to die. This awful thing was not happening to her.

With the passing days it seemed even more unreal.

Janis was back in school and zealously catching up on the work of the missed month. She played as zestfully as ever and grumbled good-naturedly about the pills she had to take on rigid schedule and the salt-free food she was limited to. She had been passionate about things like pickles and relish and fish 'n' chips, and one day improvised a doleful little poem:

> *Oh, Mommy, please call a halt*
> *To French fries with no salt!*

Neighbors made special treats for her. Once, when Mrs. Rees brought over a great batch of salt-free cookies, Janis gratefully clasped them to her and said, "Mrs. Rees, if anybody gets to heaven, I know *you* will!"

Janis ate well, drank milk in prodigious quantities, and steadily gained weight and strength.

Seemingly, everything was as it had been, yet for Rita and Rudy Babson life was irrevocably changed. Each single day had its never-to-be-repeated significance. The things they had always meant to do "sometime" with the children they now did, for "sometime" had arrived. There were long automobile trips, games and songfests in the evening—especially when Janis' uncles visited, for she was enraptured when each played his guitar—and Grandma Babson came all the way from Fort William to spend a few weeks. And always there were the secret glances at Janis, a drinking in of the way she looked and acted, and that persistent sense of unreality that this sweet and vibrant child was going to be taken away from them.

Janis had to come home from school at ten-thirty every Thursday morning so Rudy could take her to the clinic. After each visit the doctor would report the test results. Steadily, the leukocyte count fell.

Dr. English had told Rudy that if the cancer clinic sign upset Janis he would treat her elsewhere, although he preferred the hospital because of its complete facilities. But if Janis ever noticed the grim word, cancer, she never mentioned it to her father.

Nor will Rudy Babson ever forget the valiant efforts of the Ottawa Cancer Society on his daughter's behalf. "Unless you have needed these good people, you can never understand how essential they are, how sympathetic. Rich man or pauper, it's all the same—all they want to know is how they can help. I don't know how we'd have managed without them."

Janis took to her new routine avidly, and promptly made friends with all the nurses and technicians in the hematology laboratory. Offering her finger to be stuck with the needle, she grinned and told Miss Craig, "Can't you take enough for next week and save Daddy a trip?"

Janis went flitting from office to office like a busy hummingbird, greeting all hands. If she failed to see someone she knew, she tapped out a genial little message on any available typewriter:

Dear Miss Jessamyn,
    I am sorry I missed you today. Where were you?
                Love, Janis.

The hospital personnel were understandably chary of deep feelings for their little patients, especially those they knew were going to die. Yet Janis won them over in spite of themselves. One of the technicians remembered, "It's funny. We never talked about Janis when she wasn't here. I guess we just didn't like to think about what was in store for her. But around eleven o'clock every Thursday there was a sort of expectancy around here. You could *feel* it. And then, all at once, she'd be there, like a burst of sunshine."

Rarely did she miss a chance to dash up to the children's ward on the second floor and renew acquaintance with the nurses and her beloved Friedel, who managed the kitchen and invariably produced a cooky or a dish of ice cream for favored visitors. Friedel had long since been added to the interminable list of those on whom Janis asked God's blessings in her prayers. Now she came home to report solemnly to her mother that "Friedel definitely has the biggest heart in eastern Canada."

Before long, Janis knew every youngster who came to the clinic on Thursday morning. She became their guide, ally, and champion, always ready with a little joke, a word game, or the directions to the girls' bathroom. To first-timers, frightened by the alien, antiseptic smell and the glistening instruments of medicine, she was a pillar of strength, a veteran who could convincingly say, "One quick needle and you're all finished. Honest! It doesn't hurt a bit."

Janis had a good summer. During Ottawa's colorful Exhibition Week, the whole family visited the midway and all the exhibits, and Janis and Charmaine vied with each other at pitch penny and ring toss. They rode the whip and the Ferris wheel, and came off the roller coaster breathless with excitement and begging for "just one more ride." If anything, it was Charmaine whose energy and fervor were finally spent; she slept soundly all the way home, while Janis still bubbled enthusiastically over the memory of the day's sights and sounds.

On September 9th, her ninth birthday, Janis came galloping home from school filled with expectancy—to find the house strangely quiet. "Mom," she called into the empty kitchen; "Charmaine?" up the echoing stairs.

Had they *all* forgotten her birthday? Downcast, she started for her room—and had taken barely two steps when her heart leaped to the thrilling cry: "Surprise!"

They were all there—Rita and Rudy and all the kids, Tricia and her other friends, and, best of all, Uncle Joe and Uncle Bob from Montreal!

Heart on her sleeve, Janis ran from one to the other with a kiss and a fervent embrace. "Oh, I'm so happy!" she squealed.

Rita sent her to pull the drape strings "to shut that glare out." Down came a cascade of streamers and balloons, and the party was really on. It lasted until well past Janis' bedtime, filled with laughter and dancing and innumerable songs to sprightly guitar accompaniment.

Long afterward, when the little ones were finally asleep, a suddenly strained silence settled on the adults in the living room. At last, Bob Quinn spoke to his sister. "It doesn't seem possible. She's so—full of life."

"God has His reasons, I know," Rita replied softly. "I

just pray He gives Rudy and me the strength to understand them."

"You'll understand them," Bob said and, after a long pause, "Janis will help you."

The birthday gift that thrilled Janis most was a shiny new bicycle her parents had given her. Each afternoon, she set out on an exploration of the nearby woods, sometimes with Tricia or Charmaine, sometimes alone. She was captivated by the colors of fall, so vibrantly sensitive to the changing season that her return home was marked by an exuberant catalogue of endlessly fascinating discoveries she had made.

On an even footing in school again, she and Elizabeth Hayes resumed their friendly, but nonetheless ardent, competition for the top of Miss McPhee's fourth grade.

Then, in October, Janis had a setback. Her hemoglobin count dropped sharply and she was suddenly drained of energy. Dr. English reported that she was undoubtedly coming out of remission. The methotrexate had probably lost its effectiveness, he said. He prescribed another drug, 6-mercaptopurine, which worked by taking away from the rampaging white blood cells the essential chemicals needed for life. After several anxious days the new drug seemed to take hold quite well. Still, Dr. English told the Babsons, it might be a good idea if Janis were not quite so active.

Janis accepted the new restriction without fuss. "But when will this old blood of mine get better?" she asked her mother. "I've been taking the medicine for such a long time. Does Dr. English know? Will it ever get better?"

46

It was the first of many painful questions Rita Babson would have to cope with in the trying months ahead. Nor was she ever able to settle for a glib evasion. Now she took her daughter's hands and softly said, "It's a burden God has given you, sweetheart. Right now, all you can do is bear it. But someday I'm sure you'll know His reason."

And Janis, whose faith was absolute, smiled. "I know, Mom. God couldn't make a mistake. I'm just being grouchy, I guess."

So she was less active. She turned the rope for skipping games and handed out equipment during gymnasium periods and, when winter came, gazed out the dining-room window while her friends went coasting down the hill.

One afternoon, when Charmaine and Roddy were bundling up to join the fun, Janis watched with a plaintive expression. "I wish I could go out today," she murmured, then added thoughtfully, "Maybe next week I'll be able to, or the week after."

Not ten minutes later, Charmaine, impelled by some shadowy sense of guilt and a suddenly overwhelming compassion for her sister, abandoned her sleigh and came back into the house. "Brrr," she said to Janis, feigning a shudder of cold as she pulled off her coat. "It sure is nasty out. Want to play cards?"

They played until suppertime, and played with their dolls the following afternoon, both trying hard to ignore the cries of merriment from outdoors. They still had an occasional spat, but never were two sisters closer than in those days and the ones to follow.

Slowly, Janis got better again. By March when, according to Dr. English' prognosis, she ought to have been near the end of her foreshortened life span, Janis had put on weight and her cheeks were a healthy red. Her only symptom was an occasional headache.

But another, more subtle change *had* taken place. There was now a serenity about her, a quietness and a great depth. What was purgatory *really* like, she asked Rita. Were the days as long as the days on earth? Twice she reminded her parents that she wanted her eyes to go to the Eye Bank.

Always anxious to please others, it now seemed to be her greatest happiness. Miss McPhee reported to Rita that Janis was like a little mother to the younger children in school. No second- or third-grader could be jostled in the rush of playground activity without attracting Janis' quick sympathy. No tussle within her earshot could fail to draw her swiftly to the support of the underdog. She seemed to have a storehouse of pencils and notebook paper for her forgetful classmates.

Janis loved to help Rudy with the Saturday shopping for groceries, prowling around the store, looking at the shelves to find at least one item not on Rudy's list that "I'm sure Mommy needs." Time and again she would tell her parents that they ought to get out more often—"You both work so hard!"—and then would be ready with a reminder of an upcoming church dance or PTA meeting. One day, when Rita wasn't feeling well, Janis insisted on staying home from school; she cleaned the entire house expertly and made lunch for the small fry.

Early each Saturday morning, to the accompaniment of "Shhh, don't wake Mommy and Daddy," she would shepherd Timmy and Karen—and any of their little friends who came knocking on the door—down to the basement and play school with them. She taught them their letters and let them color. Sometimes, lying awake in bed, Rita could hear Janis' little girl voice in its grown-up cadences: "And now, children, because you have all been so good, I am going to read you a story. Which one would you like to hear?"

One Saturday, aglow with a brand-new idea, Janis set out to prepare a truly grand surprise for her parents. While bacon fried and Roddy stood guard at the toast-er—"Remember," she cautioned him, "it has to be golden brown!"—she dashed out front and cut the summer's first roses in the garden. Hearing the activity, Rita started to get out of bed. Rudy stopped her. "Whatever she's do-ing, she's having a good time," he said. "Let her be."

A few minutes later, carrying fancy trays, Janis and Roddy came up to present their offering with shy self-conscious smiles: it was a sumptuous breakfast—cereal with banana slices artfully arranged in a circle around the rim of the bowls, bacon and eggs, and steaming cof-fee—all embellished by two improvised rose bowls, pet-als gracefully afloat. Rudy was speechless and Rita could manage only a throaty, "Well, what's this all about?"

"You two were so worried when I was sick" Janis said. "I thought this would be a nice way to say thank you. Roddy made the toast."

She hovered over them, urging them to eat. "Does

it taste all right? I'm not so good on coffee yet, but I'm learning. Want another cup, Dad?"

The Babsons were accustomed to no more than toast and coffee in the morning. More to the point, they were both choked up with their emotions. But they ate every bite, and only allowed themselves to cry after Janis had carried the trays away.

Thereafter, Saturday breakfast in bed became a ritual offering from Janis to her parents. Later, when she would be too weak to get downstairs before them, she would say, "Oh, shucks! I had such a terrific idea for your breakfast today."

By the end of the school year Janis' blood count was absolutely normal. She hadn't had a transfusion since she'd been in the hospital, and she seemed to sparkle with health. Unable to help himself, Rudy once asked Dr. English if the improvement might not be permanent; if, indeed, the miracle had happened.

"Don't count on it, please," the doctor replied. "Be grateful she's all right now, but do me a favor: don't hope for more."

And yet, the Babsons couldn't help hoping. A new drug, perhaps, a cure—scientists were constantly making such marvelous discoveries. Hadn't they just ended the scourge of polio?

"I can't explain it," Rita Babson has said. "Rudy and I tried to make ourselves believe Janis was only on loan to us, but it wouldn't work. We both knew it was wrong and that it would only be harder in the end. But what could we do?"

Early that summer Janis suffered a great personal blow. Tricia Kennedy moved away. Her father had been transferred to the new atomic energy plant near Chalk River, and the two firm friends had to bid each other a weepy good-bye.

"I'll write every day," Tricia promised fervently. "And maybe we can visit each other, and—oh, gosh, Janis I feel so awful!"

For a long time after, Janis seemed withdrawn some-how, not quite her sprightly and buoyant self. She read a lot and talked quietly with Charmaine, but she rarely mentioned Tricia's name. Then, in mid-August, Rita said to her with sham casualness, "Oh, by the way, if you're not too busy, Tricia's coming to spend a week with you. Her father is driving her down tonight."

The gasp of utter joy, the mute gratefulness with which Janis embraced her mother were thanks enough for all the secret planning between the Babsons and the Kennedys to arrange the holiday. The two girls had a rapturous reunion and six enchanted days together, so begrudging the time for sleep that they stayed awake, whispering, far into the night. And when, at last, Tricia had to leave, both were considerably better reconciled to their separation.

Then it was September again and Janis, now ten, be-gan the fifth grade. She was delighted that Miss McPhee "got promoted, too," and was to be her teacher again. This was the year, she promised her father, that she was going to pull up her lagging arithmetic mark. She did, and also turned her pixie sense of humor loose in composition class. Describing "My Mistake in the Spelling Match," she wrote:

> I was shivering in my shoes. I could feel my knees knocking together and my teeth chattering. Then, much too soon, it was my turn. *Enthusiastically*, the teacher said, and everything in my mind went blank! I tried but I got it all wrong. I felt terrible. But guess what happened. I wasn't the only one. That word stumped every single person after me, too, and the spelling match ended in a tie!

In another paper entitled, "Me, the Mayor of Ottawa," which Miss McPhee had her read aloud, Janis prescribed some sweeping reforms indeed:

> If I were the Mayor of Ottawa, these are the changes I would make. First, the Mounted Police would have their *salury* doubled and every day that they wanted off, why they could just take it off without saying anything. Second, the girls would get anything they wanted free. Next I would have all the dirt roads paved and the potholes filled. I would make sure that every family has a TV, radio, telephone, automatic washer, drier and dishwasher. Any *juvinile delinquence* would be shot into space.

She awaited Halloween with trembly anticipation, working away for days with Charmaine to contrive wonderfully garish costumes for themselves and the small fry. Each hour was an eternity until, at last, it was time to set out "trick or treating." Out of the house sallied the young Babson contingent clad in great ghostly sheets, mop wigs, and impishly grinning masks that betrayed liberal applications of their mother's lipstick. As it grew dark Karen became frightened by some of the more wildly spooky accouterments of the other children on Cote de Neiges Road. Janis pulled off her own mask and held her little sister comfortingly. "See, it's only Dee-Dee, sweetheart. It's only a game." Thereafter, she kept the mask in her trick-or-treat bag, sacrificing the coveted Halloween illusion to keep Karen reassured that it was, indeed, only a game, and that big sister Dee-Dee was always close by.

That fall Janis became a member of the Eucharist Crusade at school, an apostleship of youngsters devoted to a *living* of the Lord's spirit. Its watchwords—pray, receive communion, sacrifice, save souls—touched Janis' deepest feelings, and she was thrilled to be elected captain of her Crusader team. Meeting days were a high point of her week, and she came away exalted, fulfilled.

Her December report card was one of her best: 100 in spelling and literature and a new high of 82 in arithmetic! "Keep up the good work, Janis," Miss McPhee wrote on the card.

But school was almost over for Janis. There were unmistakable signs that her two-year battle was taking its final turning. More blood transfusions became necessary, one every ten days now, and from time to time, Dr. English had to do additional bone marrow aspirations. Finally, she decided to resign as captain of the Eucharist Crusaders because she couldn't always get to the meetings. She was going to the clinic more often, and sometimes she and Rudy had to wait there a long time.

"It just isn't fair to the others," she sadly told the Sister Moderator. "Even when I can make the meetings at all, I come late."

Sister stroked the unhappy little girl's hair. "Never mind about being captain," she said quietly. "You can still be a Crusader, and a very special one. Suffering is more than a word to you, Janis."

It was. And worse than the physical pain now creeping up on her was a new mental anguish. The potent hormones she had been taking steadily for so many months were gradually changing her appearance. Her pert, slender face had darkened and grown heavy and bloated. The once quick-moving little body was pudgy now and awkward. In the beginning Rita tried to pretend that this wasn't really so, as much for her own sake as for Janis'. But one day at school one of the children heedlessly remarked, "Hey, Fatty, you better go on a diet!" And Janis came home crushed.

"Oh, it *is* true, Mommy!" she sobbed. "I *am* changing. The kids are ashamed even to look at me!"

Heart aching, Rita put her arms around the child and held her close. No words came to her. Silently, she prayed for guidance. "Do you think it matters so much to God how you look, darling?" she said, at last. "It's what's inside you, what you *feel*. That's what He cares about."

This seemed to appease Janis for the moment. But her spirits weren't really lifted until a Saturday afternoon a week later, when she came running into the house, then wheeled, and peered with secret excitement through the curtain.

"And what are you doing, young lady?" Rudy asked, lowering his newspaper to watch her.

"I'm playing hard to get," she replied, that inimitable grin firmly fixed on her face again. "Daddy, guess what! Ricky Lewis chased me all the way home from the school yard!"

Rudy lifted his newspaper again and whispered, "Well, bless his heart forever."

A little while later Janis' innate good humor really asserted itself. Climbing up on her father's lap, she poked his stomach and said, "I guess if I don't watch it I'll get to be as fat as you, right?"

"Who's fat?" Rudy answered, pretending to be severely affronted. "I'll have you know that's sheer muscle." And father and daughter hugged each other, laughing uproariously.

That December the St. Nicholas School sponsored a Christmas-card-selling contest. The student who took orders for the most boxes would be awarded a copy of *St. Therese and the Roses*. Janis promptly set her heart on winning, for Therese was her favorite among all the saints. She had carried the saint's tattered likeness for a year, inspirited by the serenity and loveliness of the Carmelite nun who died at the age of 24, but whose "Little

Way" to love and daily life became a lasting legacy.

But it was the same old story. By the time Janis got back from the clinic, the other St. Nicholas youngsters had already canvassed all of Cote de Neiges Road. Except for her own family and a few close neighbors, there was no one on the street left to sell cards to.

Disconsolate, Janis started up to her room. She said, "If only I didn't have to go to that darn old clinic,..." and suddenly stopped. "That's where I can sell the cards!" she exclaimed with sudden inspiration. "Why, Miss Craig will buy a box! And Miss Jessamyn and Friedel, and—oh, gosh, Daddy, when do we go again?"

In a single quick tour of the hematology lab and the children's ward she sold enough boxes to win the contest hands down—and promptly came home to read her new book straight through. Beaming, she said to Charmaine, "St. Therese is my big sister up in heaven, just like you're my big sister right here. I'm lucky."

When Charmaine asked what part of the book she had enjoyed most, Janis thought a moment, then said, "When Therese tells about her one wish: to reach the height of the mountain of love."

"The height of the mountain of love," Charmaine repeated, puzzled.

"Where God is," Janis said simply.

In gratitude for the hospital personnel's help, Janis made a little Nativity scene of cardboard and cotton batting, and took it up to the children's ward. "Would you have room for this?" she asked the receptionist.

Touched, the woman said, "Why, we'll give it the place

of honor." And she swept clear a whole corner of the information desk and, with great ceremony, installed Janis' gift.

Just before Christmas Janis' blood began to deteriorate again. Her back hurt almost constantly and the transfusions were increased to one a week in an effort to strengthen her frail body. Then Dr. English decided that it was necessary to do another bone marrow aspiration.

Janis turned white. "Please, Daddy," she begged, surrendering to fear for the first time. "I can't. I just can't!"

Rudy held her tight for a long moment. Then he said softly, "I think you can, Janis. All you need is courage—and faith."

Slowly she straightened up. She asked Dr. English and Miss Jessamyn if they would leave her alone for just a minute. Then, kneeling on the tile floor of the treatment room, she asked God for the strength to submit to the racking procedure. "I know it's necessary to make me better, dear Lord. But I do need a little extra courage."

When Rudy helped her up, he turned away so she wouldn't see how his eyes had suddenly misted.

By Christmastime the progress of the disease seemed inexorable. One night, standing over Janis' bed and looking down on the sleeping child, as she often did, Rita prayed for the miracle that would save this precious little girl. "And if there is to be no miracle, then, dear God, give me the strength to see my baby through." She covered the small foot that so persistently worked its way out from under the covers and tiptoed out.

Janis refused to give in to her aches and her weariness.

She plowed doggedly through the snow to school every day, although often Roddy had to help her back home. Her Christmas shopping was painstaking, and included secret and separate consultations with Rita, Rudy, and Charmaine. With the money she had saved from her allowance, and the extra dollar Rudy had slipped to each of the youngsters she bought a manicure set for her mother; handkerchiefs for her father—"Fathers are *so* hard to shop for!"—toys for the small fry; a pencil case for Roddy, because he was always losing his pencils; and barrettes glittering with sequins for Charmaine, who was now nearly twelve and beginning to fuss with her hair each night.

When the Babsons came home from midnight Mass on Christmas Eve, Janis was wide awake and chatting away with the baby-sitter. She was having such a gay time admiring the newly decorated tree that Rita hadn't the heart to send her off to bed. A few minutes later though, Janis was seized by nausea and a backache, and she was content to swallow a pill and let her daddy take her upstairs.

Bright and early next morning, as though she had never known pain in her life, she was down to open her presents with the other children, entranced with the pale blue party dress her parents had given her and the pleated coral skirt and sweater set Grandma Babson sent—"Just *exactly* the color I wanted!"

There was a battery-powered sewing machine for her, new paints, needlework, and lots of books for the long, grim time Rita and Rudy now knew to be just ahead. And as she sat on the floor, surrounded by wrappings and glitter, Janis said the thing that sent her mother rushing from the room: "I'll never, never have another Christmas as happy as this one!"

It was around this time that Janis must have heard something new and unsettling to her, perhaps something close to the truth, about her illness. It may have been at school or the unsuspecting remark of a neighbor; it most surely wasn't at home, for Rita and Rudy were extremely cautious in their conversations about Janis. Wherever it was, Janis came home one day pensive and lost in some private reflection. A little while later she sought out Charmaine in her room and closed the door behind her.

"What's the matter with me?" she asked abruptly, pointedly. "Am I going to get better?"

"Sure," Charmaine said automatically. "You're *getting* better, aren't you?"

"No," was the answer. "And I don't think I'm going to. You don't have to kid me."

Stunned, Charmaine stared mutely at her sister. She didn't know what to say, and she remembers a gathering sense of great fear, a tightness near her heart. Was it so? Was *that* what her mother and father had been acting so worried about all these months?

And Janis, seeing at once how her little outburst had disturbed Charmaine, was suddenly contrite, and completely shifted her ground. "Oh, forget about it," she said with a crooked smile. "I'm just being fidgety again." At the door she turned back. "Ummm—don't say anything to Mom and Daddy, okay? Forget about it."

Charmaine didn't say anything to her parents. But

she didn't forget about it, not for a long time.

A few weeks later, not long before the final bell of the school day, Janis jerked convulsively in her seat. Even as the pain in her back gathered full strength, she looked quickly around her to see if anyone had noticed. She slumped back, trying to make herself inconspicuous, gritting her teeth in silent prayer for the dismissal bell. When it came, it was all she could do to gather her books and get her coat on. And so, all unknowing, she walked out of her beloved St. Nicholas Separate School for the last time.

Roddy helped her home through fresh-fallen snow. With medication, the pain in her back eased, but Dr. English advised that she be kept at home until the weather got warmer. The severe Ottawa cold seemed to cut right through her, and she was walking with difficulty. Finally, although she was now taking antibiotics to ward off infection, her resistance was pathetically low, and even an ordinary cold could have the most serious consequences.

And so she passed the days helping her mother around the house and trying to keep up with her schoolwork. Then, one Sunday morning while Rita was getting breakfast ready, she heard a feeble call from upstairs. She dropped what she was doing and dashed for the steps. Rudy was already on his way up, and they crowded into Janis' room together—appalled by the sight of her: white-faced and arms straining alongside her, she was struggling to push herself up from the pillow, and couldn't.

"I can't," she breathed with a wan smile. "I can't even get out of bed."

They ran to her side, Rita holding her wordlessly in

60

her arms for a moment before she could manage a calm tone. "Is it that silly back of yours again, darling?" she asked. "I'm sure it will be all right in a minute."

They helped Janis to wash and to walk downstairs to have breakfast. And, indeed, it looked as though the awful numbness that had overcome her was gone. But early in the afternoon she cried out with sudden pain, as an excruciating spasm seized her back. For three full hours she writhed in silent agony, held in turn by Rudy, then Rita, neither able to do much more than mop her damp brow, rub her back, and suffer an anguish of the heart as acute as Janis' physical torture. The clinic was closed on Sundays, and the pills Dr. English had prescribed for the back pain seemed not to effect any relief at all.

Moved by the stricken look on Rudy's face, Janis whispered at one point, "Don't worry, Daddy, please. It'll go away soon."

But it was late afternoon before she could be propped up on the couch, pale and shaken by her ordeal but able to manage a weak smile. "It's better now," she said. "I'm okay."

Early next morning Rudy drove her to the clinic.

"I assume the cell mass has really spread through the spinal nerve area," Dr. English said, after he'd made an examination and done a blood count. "She'd better stay here. We'll see what we can do about that pain."

Janis made no protest when Rudy told her she would have to be hospitalized again. Her face was drawn with new pain and fatigue, but her spirit was still unvanquished. "I'm positive I'll get better sooner here," she said.

"I'll be home in a week; you'll see."

She began getting codeine for the pain, and an increase in the strength of her drugs and several transfusions soon brought her cell count into better balance. Amazingly, in three days she was out of bed and scooting from the kitchen, and her great friend Friedel, down to see the girls in hematology. Feeling quite the old hand, she went from room to room cheering up youngsters who were new to the hospital.

There was Betty, a blonde girl just Janis' age. She had been operated on for cancer. Unsuspecting, she worried only about the schoolwork she was missing, and was delighted when Janis volunteered to drill her in spelling and arithmetic. Caught getting out of bed for a book one night, Betty was roundly scolded by her new friend. "That's no way to get better! Now you get right back in there or I'll tell the nurse." Janis grinned. "I can be pretty tough, you know," she added, handing Betty the book she'd been after.

When Janis came upon a classmate, while visiting one of the other rooms on the ward, she didn't know whether to jump with glee at the sight of a familiar face or to express her regrets about his broken ankle. Her decision: to skip the amenities altogether.

"Hi," she said brightly. "Want to play cards?" They played happily until lights out time.

More than anything, Janis loved to help the nurses look after the smallest children. She would fluff their pillows, read them stories, and make funny colored pictures for them. One night she was awake until daybreak comforting Donna, a three-year-old who had been in an automobile accident and was encased in a plaster cast from toes to chin. That afternoon the floor nurses solemnly appointed Janis: "official unofficial nurse's aide." She was thrilled, and was waiting at the ward entrance at the start of visiting hours to blurt out the exciting news to her parents.

But for all her strength and depth of character, Janis was still a little girl. She knew the nurses and technicians, yet the hospital had remained a place of the adult world, and if she suspected the truth of why she was there, she kept it to herself. Now, some intimation of what lay ahead must have brushed across her mind. Sometimes she would walk down to the clinic alone and sit on a bench, a silent, wide-eyed child in a pink bathrobe, and wait for the children she had come to know through the two long years of her treatment there. But they never came.

She asked Mrs. Brown, the receptionist, "Doesn't Eddie come on Thursday anymore? And Gloria?"

And Mrs. Brown told her no, no they didn't come on Thursday anymore. Then she looked away.

One evening, soon after, Janis said to Rita, "Mom, remember Eddie and Gloria? They're dead, aren't they?"

"Yes, dear," was the softly given answer. "They are."

It was Janis who broke the long silence. Her gaze was no longer fixed on her mother, but seemed to have drifted off into the far distance. "Don't be sad," she said with quiet conviction. "They're in heaven now. They must be happy."

Miss McPhee came to see Janis and brought letters

from all her classmates. Janis was thrilled. She had to hear about each of them, and questioned Miss McPhee exhaustively. At the end, plaintive, she said, "Do you think I'll ever be able to catch up?"

"Janis Babson!" Miss McPhee exclaimed in her best teacher's voice. "I expect you to be back at the top of the class before the end of the year!" Then she bent and kissed the child, and, eyes full of tears, walked quickly out of the room.

Charmaine sent an eagerly awaited note to the hospital with her parents each evening. Once, when she skipped it, Janis said sharply, "Tell Charmaine to get with it. Doesn't she understand that I need to know what's going on at home?"

She did. The news she got from Rita and Rudy was one thing, but the kids were of her own world. Each word from Charmaine, each little trinket from Roddy or Karen was tangible assurance that she was remembered, missed. More than anything the sense of closeness to her family sustained Janis through all these long days.

She busied herself making an elaborate Valentine for Dr. English, whose daily visit was a high point of her day, and was enthralled when she got one in the mail from Ronnie, the Little Leaguer. "You were right, Mom," Janis announced as soon as the Babsons walked in that evening. "Looks are absolutely not everything!"

By the middle of February she was stronger and free of pain, and Dr. English said she could go home. "Will I be able to go back to school when the weather warms up?" she asked him.

"Unless you want to get in trouble with the Sisters for playing hooky," he joked.

In the corridor Dr. English warned Rita and Rudy about the use of codeine. "The pain will come back," he told them. "You have to keep something in reserve. Otherwise, at the end, nothing will hold her."

Back home, Janis would sit at the dining-room window, waving until the last of the neighborhood youngsters had trooped down the street to school. Then, she'd turn to a book or the mittens she was knitting for Sally. Sometimes, in the lonely afternoons, she grew restless and felt blue. "Mom," she'd call out, "forget the housework for a while and keep me company." Her favorite story, which she begged Rita to tell her over and over, was about how Rita and Rudy had met and married.

After school, friends came to visit. Invariably, from some deep and mysterious resource, Janis rallied her energy to entertain them. Once, amid peals of laughter, Rita heard one of them gasp, "Oh, Janis, please stop! I'm suffocating with laughing." Her old rival, Elizabeth Hayes, brought some schoolwork, and the two chatted together for a long time. When Elizabeth left, Janis told Rita, "They're learning to do fractions. I'll *never* catch up."

The gnawing pain grew steadily worse. It was almost constant now, and though Janis hated to speak of it, her twisted face betrayed every spasm. The codeine vials emptied more and more rapidly. Nor did even the codeine seem to be of any use when, at intervals of a week or so, Janis was stricken with a massive and agonizingly sharp attack at the base of her spine, each one more severe than the one before, each one leaving her weaker and crippling her so that every step she took called for a tremendous effort of will. Sometimes, a sharp, compulsive cry rang through the house in the dark, and when Rita and Rudy came running, Janis would apologize for waking them. "I didn't mean to yell. It just got away from me."

She always described the pain the same way. "It's as though someone were dragging a rough old tree branch through my back and pushing it down into my legs."

It became hard for her even to maintain her old enthusiasm when she went for her weekly clinic visits, although she tried valiantly. Rudy had to carry her out to the car, and she shuddered with every pothole they bounced into on the way. To spare her further torment, the girls in the hematology laboratory came out to the parking lot to take their blood specimens. Trying to make a joke, Janis asked one day, "Am I the biggest nuisance you ever had in the clinic?"

Heart aching at the sight of this once-vibrant little girl, now pathetically straining for a smile, the technician managed a muffled, "Only the sweetest." But she couldn't look up.

Even the tests were agony for Janis, for they were now forced to take up to ten separate vials and smears each time, and Janis' arms were soon pocked with scars and wounds. And one awful day they were compelled to do another bone marrow aspiration, this time injecting the shinbone.

Early on March 15th, Janis was struck with another racking session of pain in her back. It lasted into the late afternoon, her struggle with it so intense that Rita found herself desperately wishing that Janis would faint, anything to give her some respite from this unending torture. Finally Rudy called for an ambulance, and Janis was sped to the hospital.

Dr. English promptly ordered a series of massive radiation treatments. It was an extreme measure but he hoped that the X-rays might shrink the rioting block of cells concentrated at the base of Janis' spine, relieving the pain, and, perhaps, restoring some mobility to her legs.

But Janis never walked again. Instead, she was fitted with a back brace for support, and confined to her hospital bed. Still, she rarely complained and never spoke of any unhappiness. But one evening, when Rita and Rudy came to the ward for a visit, they found her dozing, a notebook open by her side. In it, she had just written this wistful record of her loneliness:

> At this moment I am crying for my dear, dear, dear mother and father as I am homesick in this hospital. I don't think I shall ever let myself think anything mean about them again in my life as right now I see how much I love them.

Rita put the notebook down. She and Rudy were badly shaken by what they'd read—and poignantly reminded that Janis' time was running out. That night they came to a decision and, in the morning, Rudy telephoned Dr. English. If he brought Janis to the hospital as often as necessary, he said, if he and Rita followed instructions explicitly, couldn't they take Janis home?

"I suppose so," English said slowly. "It's—getting late, isn't it? There isn't very much more we can do."

Charmaine and Roddy made an enormous "Welcome Home" sign. Friends brought flowers and tried to keep the house a-buzz with activity and cheer. But one of Janis' worst fears was realized: little Sally hardly knew her. Lying on the living-room couch, barely able to move, Janis would call and call, but to no avail. Once, she intentionally dropped the little statuette of the child Jesus that she had been carrying and begged, "Will you get that for Dee-Dee, please, Sally?"

The youngster permitted herself to be coaxed closer and closer until, finally, Janis could reach out and clasp her into a sweet embrace. "Oh, honey, I just want to hold you for a second. Don't you remember Dee-Dee?"

Sally began to squirm, then cry. Shattered, hurt, Janis let her go. "She doesn't even know me, Mom," she sobbed. "She's afraid of me."

"You've been away so much, dear," Rita said gently. "And she's only a baby."

"But if I die—oh, Mommy—if I die, she won't *ever* remember me!"

Stunned, Rita turned quickly away.

Rudy fixed a bed near the dining-room window so Janis could see down the street. Sometimes—and always quickly, before conscience pricked her—Rita would slip a tiny sliver of pickle into Janis' noontime sandwich, and her wan little grin of gratitude was thanks enough for this small betrayal of the doctor's orders.

Janis read a little. As long as she was able to sit up, she could still knit, slowly and with infinite patience. But, mostly, she just stared out the window and down the empty road. She tried to imagine what the woods looked like now that spring was coming, and she strained to hear an occasional shout from the school yard. But she never again asked when she might be going back to school.

The bad pain was almost always with her now. The rampaging white cells, massed at her back, were spreading from there, and had begun infiltrating her head so that her teeth ached night and day. She would bite fiercely on the little statuette of Jesus, now seldom out of her hands. Once, when Rita cautioned that she might hurt herself that way, Janis shook her head and knowingly said, "He wouldn't hurt me, Mom."

One afternoon she overheard Rita talking on the telephone to the mother of Susie, the sick little girl Janis had befriended the first time she'd been in the hospital. "How is Susie doing?" she later asked.

"She's better," was the very slow answer. "The doctors say she's going to be all right."

"I'm glad." Then, quite suddenly, Janis said, "I'm not going to get better, am I, Mom?"

Rita busied herself shifting some magazines, her heart and mind in turmoil. "Only God knows that, dear," she said at last.

This seemed to satisfy Janis. "Yes," she murmured. "He put me here and He can take me back whenever He wants to. I'm ready."

She grew worse day by day; nearly every part of her body stabbed with relentless pain. Then, around ten on a Wednesday morning in May, she was overwhelmed by another severe attack, and cried out in spite of herself: "Mommy, I can't stand it! Oh, Mommy, please!"

The codeine was no help. Frantic, Rita called Rudy and then, unable to fight it back, began to sob.

"Oh, don't do that, Mom," Janis pleaded. "I don't want to make you unhappy. I don't want that."

Rita shook her head. She was unable to speak.

"Listen," Janis whispered through tightened lips, "You helped me be brave, remember? That first time I had to go to the hospital and cried? Now it's your turn!"

"Yes," Rita finally said, and managed a smile.

They clung to each other until Rudy got home. He had already telephoned Dr. English and confirmed the inevitable: Janis would have to go back to the hospital.

As they waited for the ambulance, Charmaine came home from school. Her sister's agony and the news that she was going back to the hospital shook Charmaine severely. She wanted only to flee to her room and, behind a closed door, cry her heart out. But Janis begged her to stay downstairs, and from somewhere deep inside Charmaine found the strength she needed.

"I've got a new joke book," she said huskily. "Do you want to read it?"

"I can't. You read it to me."

And so Charmaine read jokes through blurry eyes, and by the time the ambulance came, Janis was laughing.

As the attendants were carrying her out, she asked if

they would put the stretcher down for just a moment. She looked searchingly through the house. "My last look at home," she said simply. "I don't want to forget anything. Then no one will forget me." She gazed hungrily through the window as they drove slowly up Cote de Neiges Road.

Later that evening, having examined her carefully, Dr. English found Rita and Rudy, nervous and exhausted, waiting for him in the long corridor outside the children's ward. "There's nothing else we can do," he said abruptly. "I'll see that she gets enough sedation." There was a painful pause before he added, "I told you; I'm no miracle man. I—I'm sorry. She can't last much longer." He shook his head hopelessly, plainly in the grip of a very deep emotion, and walked right past them. Rudy thought he had never seen him look so tired, so defeated.

Not long afterward Janis asked Rudy what was wrong with Dr. English. "He always used to stay and joke with me, and now he doesn't even look at me when he's here. Doesn't he like me anymore?"

"It isn't you, honey," Rudy assured her. "He's just— very busy."

And Rudy thought: it *is* too much for any man. He remembered the odd camaraderie that had sprung up between the little girl and the dedicated man of medicine in all the long months past, how the doctor's face, usually so preoccupied, lit up whenever the child marched in to his treatment room at the clinic. And now the game was up. He had done more than he had promised, but he couldn't help her any longer, and it hurt more than he dared show.

Incredibly Janis rallied again. She was getting massive doses of morphine now and, with the worst of the pain abated, her wasted little body found the strength to fight back. Two of her uncles, Jim and Joe, came to see her; and Janis who loved nothing better than company, responded with much of her old vivacity. She made them laugh with her complaints that she couldn't get a toe out from under the tight hospital sheets.

"It's like being in prison." She grinned. "I'm a girl who has to have her toes free, you know."

But Rita's brothers left Room 120 shaken men.

Next afternoon, due back in Kingston, Joe Quinn stopped at the hospital for a last good-bye. But Janis had been given some phenobarbital and was asleep. Later, learning that she had missed him, she was heartbroken. That evening, when her parents came to see her, she was dozing again, but this time there was a sheet of paper resting on her chest. "If anybody comes and I'm asleep," it said, "don't go away!!!"

When she awoke, Rita told her that her Uncle Bob was coming to see her. "I hope I don't make him as sad as I made poor Uncle Jim and Uncle Joe," she said.

Bob Quinn brought his niece an enormous paint set and sat with her all day, chatting, reading aloud to her, and, when he could, just looking at her. Toward evening Janis told him that he'd better go.

"Don't you want me to keep you company anymore?" he asked.

"Sure I do," she said with a small smile. "I wish you could stay and stay. But I've made you sad enough for one day and, besides, you look awfully tired."

She began to sink again. Even the morphine held off her pain for only a few hours, and the end was plainly near. The day after she was admitted, the hospital chaplain had given her Extreme Unction, the final sacrament of the Roman Catholic Church. Now, for the first time, she was alone in a room.

Rita has said, "I made up my mind, let the dear Lord take her if He must. Only please, spare her any more pain."

The Babsons had agreed that if there were one thing that might lighten up Janis' last days—anything, no matter how much it cost—they would buy it for her. But Janis shook her head when they asked.

"I've already cost you so much money," she said. "Besides, I really have everything I want." Then she worked her face into the shadow of a sly grin. "Anything?"

"Anything," Rudy promised.

"I'd like to see the kids again!" she said with a rush. "I know it's against the hospital rule, but maybe you could sneak Charmaine up—just Charmaine. That wouldn't be so wrong, would it?"

Next evening, Charmaine between them, Rita and Rudy slipped up a back stairway to Janis' room. "Oh, oh, oh! You did it!" Janis squealed with glee. She threw up her arms, and the sisters fell into a hectic embrace, kissing and hugging each other as Charmaine valiantly fought back her tears. She was wearing a brand-new yellow hat, and insisted that Janis try it on. They laughed and chattered away while the Babsons, who had closed the door, stood watching, achingly watching.

Janis had a parade of questions—"How's school? Do you ever see Ricky Lewis? Tell me about the small fry!"—and Charmaine was ready with a bottomless supply of anecdotes.

All unexpectedly, one of the nurses opened the door. She stopped short, took in the scene with a glance, and strode briskly to Janis' bed, handing her a pill.

"What makes you so happy?" she said off-handedly, eyes sweeping past Charmaine as though no one sat on the far side of the bed. But as she passed the Babsons on her way out, she whispered, one conspirator to others, "Better keep the door closed."

For a long time Janis and Charmaine talked on. Then, too soon, visiting hours were over. "Don't forget me," Janis said as they parted. "Don't let the little ones forget me."

Outside, the Babsons told Charmaine for the first time that Janis was going to die. And the tears she had managed to control all evening came freely now. "Why, why?" she sobbed brokenly.

Rita held her close and spoke into her ear. "Janis has accepted God's will, darling. We can't be any less brave, can we?"

"I'll try," Charmaine said, as she dried her eyes. "But I don't think I could ever be as brave as Janis."

Next morning Janis herself learned the truth. A young intern and a nurse new to the floor came into her room. "And what's wrong with you, my pretty?" the doctor asked gaily.

But before Janis could speak, the nurse, reading from

her chartbook, said, "She has leukemia."

The intern flashed her a furious look, but the damage was done. Janis lay alone until afternoon, turning that fearful word over and over in her mind. What she thought, how she faced the certain knowledge that she had a fatal disease, no one will ever know. But sometime during that long morning, she made her peace with it.

When Rita came, Janis said simply, "I have leukemia, don't I?"

Rita stood ashen-faced. She had a wild impulse to turn and flee. "What makes you think that?" she finally asked.

Janis told her what had happened.

"How would you feel if you did have leukemia?" Rita said quietly. Again she found herself drawing strength from her child's calm. "Would it frighten you?"

Janis shook her head firmly. "If that's what I have, it must be God's will that I should have it. What is there to be afraid of?" She thought for a moment, and perhaps to comfort her mother, added, "Anyhow, I might still get better, right?"

In a little while, though, she came completely to grips with herself, making a silent transition from hope to serene acceptance. Triumphantly, she said, "You know, Mom, I've been praying so hard to get better and I always wondered why I didn't. Now I know—because God didn't mean for me to get better. He wants me."

They sat together without speaking. Rita felt a great tranquility. She found herself thinking about Janis' last birthday, and how her brother Bob had predicted that Janis would help Rudy and her to find the strength to understand and accept God's will. And it was so. All these months she had been steeling herself to see Janis through this dread moment of truth. Now the moment was here, and Janis was seeing *her* through it.

"Do you remember when Susie's mother called?" Janis asked suddenly. "I was jealous. I thought: Susie is so lucky to get better. Now I see that I'm the lucky one. Susie must not be ready to go to heaven, so she gets to stay. But I'm ready, and dear God must know it."

There was no more talk of pain or medicines. Instead, in a very businesslike way, Janis spoke of heaven and the hereafter. "First," she announced, "I'm going to put my head in Our Lady's lap and ask her to console you and Daddy and look after all the kids. Then, I'll be able to relax."

Later she asked about purgatory. "Do you think I'll have to stay there long? I've got quite a few scores to settle up, you know."

Rita Babson held her little girl very close. "You've been in purgatory for over two years, darling. When dear God comes for you, I'm sure He'll take you right straight to heaven."

That evening Mrs. Rees came to visit, and Janis greeted her as "my favorite cooky baker." Mrs. Rees asked if she had finished knitting Sally's mittens, and Janis told her she still had one to go.

"Oh, you'll finish in no time," Mrs. Rees said encouragingly. "I'll help you."

Janis lifted her eyes. "I'm going to die," she said with

placid matter-of-factness. "I'd appreciate it if you finished them for me, Mrs. Rees. I promised Sally."

On Saturday, May 6th, Janis told her mother that she wanted to make a will. "People do that before they die, don't they?"

"Yes," Rita said after a long pause.

Noting her mother's unhappiness, Janis said, "Please don't be sad, Mommy. That's the one thing that bothers me, that you and Daddy will be sad. You still have the other kids. And I'll be there whenever you need me, honest I will."

Rudy suddenly rose and went to stand outside the door, overcome by a tremendous surge of emotion. Silently, he listened as, inside the room, his daughter made preparations for her long last journey.

"... my new bike is for Charmaine, and my paint set to Roddy—poor Uncle Bob, he spent so much money for it!"

Sitting there writing, Rita again had that sudden flaring sense of unreality. None of this was true, she thought. It just wasn't happening. It was a nightmare and she could wake up if she really put her mind to it.

But she went on writing stoically in a notebook as Janis dictated. She asked that her brace be given to some other child who might need it — "It's practically new!"— and that Friedel be told where she was buried, in case she wanted to visit the grave. "Give Daddy my prayer book and piggy bank, and I want you to have my bath salts. And, Mommy, please don't forget about the Eye Bank!" She paused. "Let's see, I guess that's all."

Rita walked quickly to the hospital chapel to pray.

On the morning of May 10th, Rita brought Janis a new picture of St. Therese. Janis gazed at it tenderly. "She's smiling on this one," she said softly. "She's expecting me."

Soon she was drifting in and out of coma. An oxygen tent had been placed over her head to ease her breathing, and the nurses were instructed to give her morphine as often as necessary. But it had little effect on the pain now. It was all between Janis and her relentless adversary.

"Mommy," she said once, "this is Ascension Day, isn't it? Wouldn't it be wonderful to go to heaven on the same day our Lord did?"

Across the hall someone was playing a radio, and one of the nurses stopped in to ask if Janis wanted it turned down. Rita was about to say "Yes" when Janis shook her head feebly. "I love it," she whispered, and tried wriggling her toes in time to the music. With a last trace of that impish grin, she said, "If only these darn sheets weren't so tight, I could really beat it out."

Later she asked if she could be buried in her new party dress, then thought better of it. "That's selfish, Give it to Charmaine."

"It wouldn't fit Charmaine, dear," Rita told her.

"Oh, in that case …" And she drifted off for a moment.

Janis didn't die on Ascension Day. Rudy stayed on through the night, while Rita went home to get some rest. He held his child's hand and stared fixedly at her face, now in repose, now twisting with sudden hurt. Once she woke and asked if it was past midnight. When he told her that it was, she said "God's not ready yet."

Rita came early Friday morning, May 12th. A nurse, who had plainly been crying, stopped her in the corridor. "Please tell her how nice she looks," the nurse said. "It hurt her so, but she wanted us to—get her ready."

She told Rita how Janis had asked the nurses to "pretty me up." They had washed and combed her hair, although each touch and movement was agonizing to the child. Then she'd insisted on wearing her new pink nightgown with the tiny white flowers. They had had to slit it up the back to get it on her.

"Oh, you look just lovely, darling," Rita said when she walked in.

Janis smiled. She was clear-eyed but very weak. "I'm ready any time now," she said. "But I'd like you and Daddy to stay with me."

She told them she had a feeling that she would not die until it grew dark. "Death is like the night," she said, "all quiet and peaceful."

She had remembered that it was Karen's birthday, and asked if it was a nice day. Rita told her it was.

"I'm glad," she said. "At least she has that—I've kind of spoiled her fun." She smiled. "I don't even have a present for her. I guess you'll just have to give her a kiss for me."

She drifted off, woke, slept again. Once she asked Rita if she could be weighed after she died. "I want to know if I'm going to heaven the way I used to be—nice and thin."

"Your body is only a—dress, darling, for here on earth," Rita said. "Anyhow, how could I tell you?"

Janis laughed aloud. "Of course! I'm getting dumb in my old age." She closed her eyes. "But you will dress me nicely, won't you? And put a pretty ribbon in my hair?"

In the late afternoon, as though struggling up out of a bad dream, she opened her eyes and spoke very clearly. "Daddy! Have you made the arrangement with the Eye Bank?"

Stricken, Rudy admitted that he had not.

"You promised me! I want you to do it now. Please." Even in her husky whisper, the Babsons sensed the essential toughness of her.

Now Rudy exchanged a look of raw pain with Rita. They had talked a great deal about Janis' persistent request. They never for a moment doubted that it was more than a mere whim, or that they'd be haunted with guilt if they failed her. But, as Rita put it, "Here was this little tyke who'd give away anything she owned to make someone else happy—even her eyes. But did she really understand? Would she be scared later? We just couldn't bring ourselves to do anything that might make the end harder for her."

And now, in that exchange of glances, the Babsons knew. Janis *did* understand. She wasn't scared. And this was the gift that, above all, she wanted to bestow.

Rudy went out into the hall, not certain why. For it suddenly came over him that he just didn't know what to do. How do you go about giving a loved one's eyes to the Eye Bank? Who do you tell? How much time do they need?

One thing Rudy Babson knew beyond doubt: of time there was not much to spare. And, having made his promise, he *had* to keep it.

Anguished, he hurried to the floor nurse's desk. "Miss Chapman," he began uncertainly, "Janis—she has this idea about giving her eyes to the Eye Bank when she's—gone. I don't know how to—I . . ." He broke off, shaking his head helplessly. "I promised her, but now I don't know what to do," he said.

Miss Chapman touched his arm. "I'll phone Dr. English," she said. "We'll arrange it, Corporal Babson. Tell Janis not to worry."

Rudy went back to the room and said it was all taken care of. Janis smiled gratefully. "Thank you," she breathed.

In an hour an intern had come with a form for Rudy to fill out and sign. "That's all there is to it," he said. "Thanks—and thank Janis."

By 9:00 P.M. Janis was so weak that she made no more effort than to open her eyes from time to time to look from Rita to Rudy. Content that they were close by, she would sigh and slip off again.

Then, quite suddenly, she struggled to sit up. Her eyes were wide and staring straight ahead, as though she couldn't see enough of what stretched before her.

"Oh, is this heaven?" she called out. "Mommy! Daddy! Come quick!"

They bent to her, held her, amazed at the sudden strength in the wasted little arms pulling them into a last embrace. And then there was no strength at all.

A moment or so later Miss Chapman's telephone rang. It was Jim Quinn. Back in Montreal, it had occurred to him that a long-distance call might cheer up his niece. He explained this to Miss Chapman and asked if she could plug a phone in at Janis' bedside.

"I'm sorry," Miss Chapman said brokenly. "Janis has just died."

It was 9:25 P.M.

Numb, Jim Quinn put the receiver down. He began to cry. But in a little while, he had pulled himself together, thrown some things into a bag and started driving back to Ottawa. He pulled into the stucco house on Cote de Neiges Road only a little while after the Babsons, stunned and silent, had returned from the hospital, and he helped them through the next difficult hours, their first without Janis.

By that time Janis' precious eyes were on route to Eye Bank headquarters in Toronto. Today, somewhere in Canada, two people can see again because a little girl they never knew insisted on giving one last gift of herself.

Most of the five hundred-seat St. Augustine's Church was filled on the day of Janis' funeral. All the St. Nicholas Separate School was there, as she had asked that they be. Elizabeth Hayes sobbed throughout the service and had to be held and comforted by Miss McPhee, who was herself weeping bitterly.

But Janis lay serene and lovely. She wore the pale blue party dress, and the pert velvet ribbon tied in her hair would have delighted her.

"Janis was anxious to be with God in heaven," said her pastor, Reverend Frederick Brossler, in his touching eulogy, "though she was broken-hearted to have to discontinue school, for she wanted so much to finish the grade with the rest of the class. Well, a happy and peaceful journey to you, Janis. You have graduated with highest honors."

The Babsons came home from the cemetery uplifted somehow. Janis' short life would always be unique and wonderful to them, of course. But they sensed something more, an answer to their grieving question—why—although they did not yet know what it was. Her Uncle Bob Quinn put it this way" "That child's ten years on this earth are not all there is to it. It can't be."

It wasn't. In Deep River a local reporter was interviewing a newly arrived family for a meet-your-neighbor page. They were the Kennedys, formerly of Cote de Neiges Road. He asked if they had any human interest stories to round out his copy.

"I have," Tricia piped up, and told how her best friend, Janis Babson, dying of leukemia, had pledged her eyes to the Eye Bank.

The reporter telephoned columnist Tim Burke of the Ottawa *Journal*, and Burke went to see Rita and Rudy Babson. His poignant story was picked up by the Canadian wire services. A few months later a nun was so moved by Janis' courage that she wrote a touching memoir, called *Janis of City View.*

The ripples continued to spread. Letters began descending on the modest little house on Cote de Neiges Road, including some from members of Parliament, one from Ottawa's mayor, Charlotte Whitton, and one from RCMP Commissioner, C. W. Harvison. Most touching were those from youngsters whose teachers had read them

Janis' inspiring story. Typical was one from Clandonald, Alberta:

> Dear Corporal and Mrs. Babson:
> How are you? I am sorry Janis died. How are Charmaine and your other children getting along? Our whole class cried when we heard the part where Janis died. You must be very proud.

To this day Rita and Rudy try to devote an hour or so each evening to answering the letters that still come from all parts of North America. In Toronto a retired druggist named Abe Silver was so touched by Janis' story that he established the Janis Babson Memorial Endowment Fund at the Hebrew University in Jerusalem for prizes in leukemia research.

But most remarkable was the phenomenal—and continuing—growth in pledges to the Eye Bank. On the day Janis died, and back to 1959, when records began to be kept, a total of 644 Ottawans had promised their eyes at death. In the two years since, there have been 1,710 *more* pledges, including all the Babson family!

It began the very day after Tim Burke's column appeared in the *Journal*. Before the Eye Bank office closed, 27 donors appeared to sign pledges. It was a one-day record—and was almost immediately broken when, at a meeting of the local Kinsmen Club, 50 members spontaneously rose to will their eyes. Not long after, a delegation of 175 from RCMP headquarters including Mounties, their families, and other employees did the same.

And so it has gone. Thereafter—and to the present day—Ottawans, individually and in clusters of from ten to a hundred, inspired by the grace and goodness of a little girl, have taken the step which someday will bring sight to many hundreds of blind men and women. Today, on a per-capita basis, Ottawa leads all Canada in the number of Eye Bank donors.

And perhaps Janis' final gift is that the Babsons can treasure her memory without the hollow grief that sometimes makes the sound of a departed loved one's name a cause for fresh sorrow in the family's hearts. "She had a mission," Rita Babson said recently, "and so she had to leave us. But I feel her presence very strongly, as though she were sitting right here, on this couch."

Charmaine tells of the day the family went to choose a headstone for Janis' grave. "You spell Janis with an 's,'" Rita told the engraver, when they'd made their choice.

"Yes, and you'd better get it right," Roddy added. "Janis was pretty tough about that; she'd be just the sort to come up and scratch it all out, if you got it wrong."

She is buried in Notre Dame Cemetery, not far from the road. "She's close to all the activity," Rudy said, "which is just where she'd want to be." The family visits there almost every Sunday, and then Janis' buoyant spirit is very much with them.

When Rita called Friedel to tell her of Janis' wish, that Friedel know her place of burial, and learned that the cook had unexpectedly gone to California to live, she felt quite badly. Janis had been so explicit about wanting Friedel to know where she was. Then, not long ago, Friedel came back to Ottawa for a visit and got in touch with the Babsons. When she went out to Notre Dame Cemetery to visit the grave, the final provision of Janis' will had been fulfilled.

Lately Sally's hair has begun getting darker. She is nearly four now and she looks amazingly the way Janis did at that age. To her, Janis is very much alive. She talks to her picture and, on Sunday, bustles the family into getting ready for their regular cemetery visit, "so we can see Dee-Dee."

Janis forgotten? She remains, as she promised she would, very much a part of the Babson household and of the life she loved so much.

ABOUT THE AUTHOR

Larry Elliott wrote his first magazine article in 1948 and his first book in 1963. Now he uses a Mac instead of a Remington upright, but he is still writing. A New Yorker born and bred, he served in the Pacific theater during World War II but, soon after, visiting his hometown became only an occasional luxury. In thirty years as a Reader's Digest Roving Editor, he has covered stories from Mexico to Moscow and from Alaska to Australia, spent at least one night in each of the United States and all the Canadian provinces, and visited thirty-five other countries on five continents. He is the author of ten books, among them biographies of Pope John XXIII, New York's Depression Mayor Fiorello La Guardia and an Alaskan Indian named Jim Huntington.

Larry Elliott has children (four) and grandchildren (five) living on both American coasts, but he and his wife Gisèle are longtime residents of the Grand Duchy of Luxembourg, where he has been twice decorated.

CPSIA information can be obtained
at www.ICGtesting.com
Printed in the USA
LVHW092027230223
740261LV00040B/696